"The beauty and wisdom in these poems amazes me. This is such powerful material it is giving me 'happy chills'. I was so excited as I continued on and finished reading Helena's second book in this series. I can hardly wait to get to her next book."

— *Agnes L. Kirby, Scriptwriter and Poet*

"This book is Brilliant! The messages and lessons are so simple, yet so powerful. I found I continuously needed to set the book down and ponder the wisdom of the words I had just read. I can't wait to indulge in the other books in the *Purposeful Mind Series*."

— *Lisa Francis, Online Marketing*

"ILLUMINATION was such an inspiration to me. I loved the poem titled *Discussion with My Higher Self*. That is the space and place I am in at this moment. *Get Rid of the Veil* was very powerful for me — I have been wanting, feeling, needing, to 'go home' for a very long time! And, it goes without saying that I loved *Unearth Your Starry Origins* & *The Experiment Goes On*. So enjoyable and mind opening! Reading this book was a time of resonance for me. I would recommend it to anybody who is interested in accelerating their evolution and understanding their origins."

— *Sally Parsons, Reiki Master, EFT Practitioner, Artist, facilitator, speaker, teacher*

"ILLUMINATION is a collection of heartwarming poems that those on a spiritual path can surely relate to. It offers a soulful glance at who we really are, our true identity. When we wake up to that truth, life here on Earth makes sense, and eternity takes on deep new meaning."

— *Anna C. Younge, Marketing*

"ILLUMINATION invites us to wake up and become one, to be in tune with our soul. Only then can we journey to that place of awareness, fulfillment, freedom, and joy. Take time to explore and savor the insightful depths that this lovely book offers."

— *Jeane Watier, Award Winning Author*
of Visionary Fiction

ILLUMINATION

Getting to Know the Invisible You

Purposeful Mind Series – Book Two

Other Books by Helena Kalivoda

AWAKEN!
Spirit Is Calling

WAKE UP!
Your Heart Is Calling

WAKE UP!
Prosperity Is Calling

Purposeful Mind Series:

CREATION
Accessing Your Untapped Potential

ILLUMINATION
Getting to Know the Invisible You

CONTEMPLATION
Understanding Your Inner World

EVOLUTION
It Is Time for the New You

METAMORPHOSIS
What Else Is Possible?

ILLUMINATION

Getting to Know the Invisible You

Purposeful Mind Series – Book Two

HELENA KALIVODA

AUDRENAR BOOKS

ILLUMINATION
Getting to Know the Invisible You
Purposeful Mind Series – Book Two

Copyright ©2012 by Helena Kalivoda
Published by Audrenar Books

Library and Archives Canada Cataloguing in Publication

Kalivoda, Helena,
Illumination / Helena Kalivoda.

Poems.
ISBN 978-0-9877521-1-6

I. Title.

PS8621.A469I45 2012 C811'.6 C2012-902413-9

Editing: Agnes L. Kirby
Cover art: original oil painting by Jaroslav Kalivoda

For more information on this book and other books by Helena Kalivoda visit www.awakenbyhelena.ca.

*I am dedicating this series to my family
and to all who are searching to reconnect
with that part of divinity we call Self.*

CONTENTS

ACKNOWLEDGEMENT

I am thankful to Spirit for transmitting this remarkable material to me. A further thank-you goes to Agnes L. Kirby for her thoughtful help while editing this Purposeful Mind series of five books. My appreciation goes to my husband for understanding my need for the prolonged periods of time that I have spent writing. Thank you all, my incarnate and spiritual muses, for your presence in my life. I am very grateful.

Helena Kalivoda

PREFACE

In this second book of the *Purposeful Mind* series, I am inviting you on a journey of self-discovery through connecting deeply with your Spirit Self.

Illumination is a discourse on the *invisible*, on that part of humanity that is hidden from our three-dimensional senses. The book delves into subjects such as our God within, our Thee (our Oversoul), our being the energy of Oneness, humanity's relationship with the stars and more.

The timeless wisdom of these powerful motivational verses will lead you home, to your Self. They will inspire you to fulfill your potential through understanding your dual nature.

I have been receiving guidance from the Spirit world for over fifteen years, and I wish you as much enjoyment from these verses as I received when transcribing, that which came to me from the ethers.

Helena Kalivoda

YOU AS GOD

YOU ARE AN EVERLASTING GOD

Below and above, left and right is God,
God of an everlasting value.
God is your strength you can depend on
in illness and grief.
Forever God is.
He is in you and is known to you.
He is all around you. He is.

God is, was and will be,
as he is all that you see.
God is an invisible net
that is bonding all together.
God is an omnipresent power.

That is not to say
that you cannot have a good day
if you believe in God.
You are about to burst out laughing
and then you stop to say
oh, and what about God?

Oh no, no, no.
Feel free to smile, jump, and roar.
Feel free to make waves and uproar.
Feel free to persist in what you are.
Feel free to continue who you are.

Yourself is what you are looking for.
Yourself is what you need to be.
Yourself is you and no one else.
Yourself is all that you have.

It is not about discouraging yourself.
It is about knowing yourself.
It is the feeling of freedom
that engulfs you when you find
that you are what you are, God.
God who is omnipotent, everlasting
like you, as you are God.

BELIEVE THAT GOD IS IN YOU

Home is the place of your origin,
a place of indescribable beauty.
Home is where horses roam free,
where birds sing at all times,
where people wake up
from a prolonged sleep called life,
their life on Earth.

Living on Earth does not preclude knowing
who you really are.
But it is difficult to carry on
those beliefs, that knowledge,
when reincarnations continue
and continue on.

Reincarnation is a way
of resolving unresolved issues.
Repeated incarnations are the prolonging
of life on Earth for reasons
such as not understanding your encumbrances,
not understanding your goal,
not understanding that you are a Soul.

A Soul is you. You are a Soul. A Soul is yours.
Which is which?
All are true. All are valid,
as without the Soul you would not exist
and the Soul could not be anything without you.

Dilemma is when you forget who you are.
Dilemma is when you forget that you are a Soul.

The Soul is a means of being God to you.
The Soul is a minuscule part
of a big, big consciousness called God.

God, as the Soul within you, is impoverished
if you do not recognize your Soul properties
which incline you toward gentleness and beauty,
open relations with nature, singing, creating
and truly believing that God is in you, within.

GODDESS WHO IS RESPLENDENT

Lethargy is the devil's way of saying
you have time, don't worry.
If you have not managed,
there are other lifetimes
and you will succeed eventually.

What's the rush, you may say.
What is this all about?
Well, let me just give you an account
of what transpired through millennia.

You were born eons and eons ago.
You were one of the little stars
that put on a flesh garb
and started your incarnation cycles.

You were born many, many times.
You were crass and of a high class.
You were all and everybody
under the sun.

You were a mother and a father.
You were a brother and a sister.
You were uncles, lovers, aunts,
children and grandchildren.

You have seen all facets of life.
You were a miser and a beggar.
You were of a high upbringing.
You were anything and anybody.

Now it is time to bring it together.
Now it is time to reclaim your own nature.
Your own mediocre, high, priestly, vain,
all mixed together nature, and then claim
your right to the Kingdom of God.

You are that God. You are that Goddess.
You are the Goddess who is so resplendent.
You are the master of your own Universe.
You are the one, who is in charge,
in charge of your own destiny.

Do make a plan. A plan that will take you
from where you are today
to the blueprint that you discarded on your way
through this material world,
where you busied yourself with earthly matters
to the point of forgetting who you were.

There is an abode, an abode of wisdom,
of calm, peace and respect for yourself,
an abode that is within.

There is a shrine that you need to discover,
as you may need to recover
to become the one who is wise,
who is not gullible but also is not crass.
Who is a balanced, a shining example to those
who are bearing the cross,
the cross and joy of humanity.

Be at peace with yourself and all others.
Be at peace.

24

You, God and Goddess who are within you,
you, please come home.
We have been waiting for so long.
Do come back and join for a little intermezzo
of brotherly and sisterly love.

YOUR SOUL IS YEARNING TO GO HOME

You are a star that is shining
and insofar, as we can tell,
you will find the link with the Universe again.
The link that is buried but not entirely lost
in the arid, arid memories of yours.

Please do come back, do.
You have been paying
a big price for the years of neglect,
neglecting your Soul, your godly being,
neglecting your Soul.

The earthly body is a mere temporary shell.
The earthly body is yours to keep and shed
once you realize that you are a Soul.
A Soul that is vibrating in all of you.
A Soul that is your lighthouse to guide you
through days and nights of your earthly lives.

Your earthly lives are your burden
that is not quite so heavy,
as you are enjoying the senses
that keep you happy.
Is that happiness of yours the happiness
that is all encompassing you,
you and your Soul?

Your Soul is yearning to go home.
Your body is worried about letting it go,
as your body knows
that without the Soul it is helpless.

It is helpless like a little child
that depends on the care of his mother.
And the child knows that he will grow up.
The child knows that he will eventually go,
go away from his mother's home.

Your Soul is calling to you.
Let's go, let's go home.
Let's go where we belong.
Let's go where there is another life
that is eternal,
and where glory is given to our creator
God.

Those yearnings are not a whim
for an untouchable, unreachable God.
Please understand that God is within.
He is within you, he really is.
He is the Light that guides you.
He is the Light that is calling you.

Come back, come back.
Do not lose another day of toil on Earth,
which is your mother now.
Do realize that you belong here,
here with us, with the stars.

Come and be with us, who are oh, so near
but far away in your mind.
Be with us, your brothers and sisters,
who have been waiting and still are.

GOD IS ALWAYS READY TO MEET YOU

God is an omnipotent power.
God is you, us, all within and around you.
Mountains, streams, birds, fish,
all sentient and inanimate things,
all is God.

God is a given. God is not a story
made up to heal wounds.
God is real. God is and will be.

God is within, is so close and yet far away.
God is impeccable in her own way.
God is unreachable, if you so decide.
God is always ready to meet you halfway.

Halfway is easy, if you are ready to move.
Halfway of God is always there.
It is you, who needs to take a step
to get somewhere.

It is you who is welcomed by God,
who watches your attempts and your fear.
God is always clear
about your intentions.

He is God omnipotent, loving.
He is God.
She is Goddess fertile, creative.
She is Goddess.

God and Goddess is one.
God and Goddess are one.
God is Goddess and Goddess is God.

THE WAY TO GOD

God is, was and will be. So are you.
You are in his image and that is far,
far from saying that you are God.

Then what is God, where is he hiding?
Where is she hidden?
Where has he been all this time?

Oh God, you elusive dear God,
do show me your face.
Do tell me where is that place,
where is it you are hiding?
Oh God, God, I yearn to know you.
Oh God, God, I yearn to meet you.

I am at your service
and I am one with you.
I am ready to be initiated
into your Kingdom
that is vast and beautiful,
that is solemn and rich in colour,
that is peaceful and restful.
Oh God, do show me your face,
please show me your face.

The way to God is to be peaceful,
to be love and wisdom,
to be quiet and at rest,
to be like a garden that is full of zest,
full of colours, sounds and lovely smells
of the Garden of Eden.

The Garden of Eden, of Adam, of Eve,
of those, who like us, you and me, are here.
Here and there and everywhere,
and are ready to enter through this big wide door.

The door that is wide open to those who know
but hidden to those who cannot tell
a God from a dream, a river from a stream,
a flute from an oboe.

YOU ARE CONSCIOUSNESS

You are consciousness.
Humans call consciousness God.
You are becoming what you already are,
you are on the way. How?
By being calm and peaceful, and always ready
to drop all for God's presence,
the presence of the omnipotent consciousness.

You are beginning to understand.
Your understanding is not based on your mind.
Your understanding is coming from your heart.
Your heart that can be full of sorrow,
your heart that will heal tomorrow,
the heart that is broken today
but will be celebrating soon.

Soon, soon, the bliss will be here.
Soon, soon, the bliss will enter
your body, your mind,
your kind, pretty and wonderful body.

Body that is expecting God.
Body that is getting ready to give up
all that is earthly and material,
all that is not of heaven,
for all that is quite formidable,
as it is, and has been for millennia,
as it is, and has always been.

ARE YOU PERESTROIKING?

You are not doing that well
if you are procrastinating at all times,
if you are a creature of those habits
that are not too conducive,
and you are suspended and waiting
for some outer signs.

Outer signs are not what you need to see.
Inner guidance is what you need.
Inner guidance is a gift you need to cultivate.
Inner guidance is a guide
that is true and well tried,
that is a lighthouse in the dark.

Your post on Earth is of a short duration.
Your post is a short-lived occasion
of a very, very important stage,
as this is where you hone your skills,
as this is where you procrastinate or get going.

Earth is a place of reckoning
with your fears,
with your anomalies,
with your futile attempts,
with your amazing successes,
with all your everlasting urges
to join your maker, God.

God within you is crying to get out
to be with you all the time,
to be in tune with you on an ongoing basis

when you talk to him and listen,
all at the same time.

Dilly-dallying is not going help you.
Why not plunge yourself into
what you really desire?

Without dilly-dallying, all is prospering,
and with dilly-dallying all is lifeless.
Simply speaking, if you procrastinate,
you will not conquer yourself.

God is within. God is not outside of you.
God is you and is not dilly-dallying
to conquer you.

God is driven if you are.
He is asleep if you are.
God is your first friend
if you want to have one,
and he is not
if you do not care to have one.

Are you doing what you need to?
Are you perestroiking[1] your own ado?
Are you perestroiking?

I am not. I am not too refined.
I am not living a saintly life.
I am of a coarse nature.

---

[1] Perestroika is a Russian word for reconstruction, restructuring. Perestroika was the name for the programs that began to reform the economy of the former U.S.S.R. in 1987.

Who says that?
Is it you? Is it your ego?

You are a beautiful creature.
You are a song that is heard.
You are a perennial flower.
You are a critter of nature.
You are manly and womanly.
You are, you are.

You are what you are.
You are love.

YOUR GOD WITHIN YOU IS CALLING

God is an omnipotent being
that is pure energy.
God is an omnipotent vital energy
flowing through all in existence.

You were God at the beginning,
as you split from a thing
called the primordial mass,
primordial mass of stewing energy
called God.

Your God within you is calling.
Listen to the call
through being gentle, open, honest,
and endeavouring always to extend
a helping hand to those
who cannot do better at the moment
as their vision is clouded,
as their vision is smeared
with material greed generated by fear.

Understand that you are God.
Understand your godly nature.
Be, flow, exist as God does.
Be free, without fears and greed, without doubts,
with an understanding that you, God,
you are creating what you are.

Through love, through abandonment to joy.
Through bestowing your love and joy on others.
Through loving your sisters and brothers.

Through plainly stating what is on your mind
when you can see where the others are—
when they are not able to understand
their own grandness.

BECOME A KING

YOUR SPIRIT IS VAST

This day is your victory day.
Take the control into your hands.
You are of Spirit and Earth—
make this day a day of reckoning
with your dual nature.

Come to realize the power you have.
You are a decision maker,
you are a story maker
of the story of your own life.

Life is not what you may think,
as you can change it in a blink,
by your thought, by your thinking,
by appreciation of yourself,
by action in the present time
that will shape the future at all times.

Your Spirit is vast and is beautiful.
Your Spirit is vast and is plentiful.
Your Spirit is vast and is full of all
that is not of Earth,
and above all, it is steeped in the reality
of Kings[2] and Queens[2], of Kings and Queens.

---

[2] The author believes that this is in reference to the Kingdom of God, to our Divine presence, and also to humanity's coming evolution of becoming "Christed"—meaning, humans will open to the higher nature of themselves to become self-realized.

BECOME A KING

You are becoming a King.

A King is a person who is steady.
Steady, in his manners.
Steady, in his beliefs.
Steady, in showing love to all around.
Steady to help and give a helping hand
whenever there is a need,
whenever there is an opportunity
to conquer greed.

A King is a person with loving ways,
with loving attitudes that are the rays
of hope for all around him.

A King is a person
who knows the laws of the Universe,
who lives the laws of the Universe,
who does not pretend that all is the same,
who understands the quiver of hate and joy,
who is in control
of his own, very own, destiny.

A King is a person that is purposely
giving himself to God
through living the godly thoughts
of exuberance, of joy, of a medieval Light
that comes through the might of God.

A King is not beleaguered by others.
A King understands that his brothers
are all striving in their own way
to reach out far beyond them,
to touch the core of their being,
to touch the stars,
to be close to God
at all times.

A King is a person that is close to self-realization.
A King is a person
about to take a journey, a flight,
that will take him to his might
of discovering the source of Light
that keeps on shining and calling.

The purpose of life is to become a King—
a King, the true warrior for truth and beauty,
for indescribable joy and happiness
that the Universe is full of
and is giving to us to use it as we want,
as we want.

Our will creates what we are.
Our will is giving us powers to become,
to become a King, a warrior of God.

YOUR KINGDOM COMES

The harps are playing and you can hear
their wonderful, wonderfully clear
tone that is beckoning you.
Pristine sounds of the Universe.
Pristine, beautiful sounds
oblivious of any earthly chords,
of any earthly music,
of any earthly minds.

We are asking you to consider meditation
as part of your evolution
toward the stars,
toward the echelons of angels and archangels,
toward the promise of a day
when you rediscover that you may
plant the seeds of your hope
and also seeds of friendships.

These seeds will grow and grow
and will be a big throwback to those
who think that there is not a King
and there is not a Soul.

Who is a King?
A King is a person who can see
beyond the earthly views and images.
A King is a person who will
discard the old notions
of the physical world at will
and will be totally prepared to direct his destiny.

"Our Kingdom comes" literally means
that you too shall become a King
and will follow the trail
of those who reached the Kingdom
when the perplexing question
of "who am I?" is answered.

THE MARK OF A KING

Do not employ sad thoughts.
Do not employ black, unruly ideas.
Do not preserve your old hurts and hates.
Clear yourself of all encumbrances.
You will be a new person,
you will be entitled to your kingdom—
your Kingdom of God.

The game of senses may be alluring,
however, the senses are a passing thing.
Senses are not all you possess.
You are a Spirit. Do not forget,
a Spirit is what you are.

You are not, repeat, you are not a bag of flesh.
You are not ready to abdicate, die and decay.
You are a living organism that is evolving,
and, from fraternizing with like-minded people,
are influenced and influencing them.

Pristine thoughts and a pristine mind
are the mark of a King
who can always be recognized by his kin,
who can always be recognized.

ANY TIME HE CHOOSES

Away from mother Earth.
Away from father Moon.
Away from human clothes.
Away from human droves.
Away from human skin.
Away from humans who are akin
to those who cannot yet understand
the glory of becoming a King.

Who is a King, who is he?
Is he you or is he me?
Perhaps you need to know
the King is the one who can leave his body
to visit the Universe.

He visits any time he chooses.
He visits any time he feels like.
He visits and visits.
He comes back and comes back
any time, any day, any sun, any May,
any, any time.

THAT DAY IS VERY NEAR

Please contemplate from the morning 'til dawn.
Be one of the many who will cross the line,
the lines of invisible threads
that are snaking between the worlds.

What does it mean?
Will it be a dream?
Will it be sudden?
Will others who stay behind notice
that you are gone?

Not at all my dear, not at all.
It will not be a pole, south or north,
a negative or positive charge.
It will be all invisible,
as the thread is thin
and the difference is very dim.

All will happen that you will know.
You will know that you know.
You will be aware,
you will not ask the questions
that you do today.
You will not be asking the questions
that are easy when you know
and hard if you don't.

Let's just say,
be aware that day is near, very near.
You will be that sure, as we are sure.

You will be happy, as we are.

You may feel obliged to say,
I don't know, oh well, what day
will this thing happen anyway?

It is here, the day is near.
You will be sure when it comes.
You will be, oh yes, you will trust
your intuition at all times.

Please listen well,
that day, that day is here.
It is that day that you will be anointed
a Saint, a King, who is aware,
a Saint that can play
any music any time,
as he knows where the buttons are,
what he can pull and push
to give out this very lush,
very lush, strong, beautiful sound
of music, of God,
of God coming down
to meet his new lamb.

A new lamb that is returning home.
A new lamb that is releasing its Soul to God.
And that day is here, that day is near.
That day is a beautiful, beautiful awakening.

ALLOW YOURSELF TO BLOSSOM

Please inherit the steeple.
Not a steeple like in a church,
a church that is old and dark,
that needs to be lightened up
to illuminate instead of frighten.

A church that will be for people.
A church with a long, long steeple
that will reach all the way to heaven.

Heaven, as in a Universe.
Heaven, as in energy.
Heaven, as in blues and reds.
Heaven, like a synergy
of material and spiritual.

Please allow yourself
to blossom into a spiritual being.
A being that has been fulfilling her destiny.
A being that is discovering the truth.

You are the children of the Universe,
not of the Earth.
You are the children of the Universe.
Yes, you are.

HE WAS A KING

There was a King, a King of two worlds.
He was a King, and in a wink
he was gone and his attire
changed from red to green.

He was the traveler that spanned two worlds.
He was the group that was not a group.
He was one and he was many.
He played and played his songs and tunes
and also said some runes.
He was a King, he was a King.

And the story says he was a King.
He was the one who knew
that he would live until the days were anew
with the glory of him becoming a King again.

A King of all spaces, a King of all places,
and he was a King of two worlds.
Who was this King, do they know?
Was he a pauper? Maybe.
They don't know.
Was he rich or wasn't he?
Well, they don't know, as he was thy Thee.

He was thy Thee, You, and Me.
The King of two worlds,
two worlds that differ,
two worlds that are the same.

ONCE A KING, ALWAYS A KING

Once a King, always a King.
A King? What does it mean?
Who and what is that King?

You will become a King
as you will be driven by a desire
to expose your roots, your previous attire.

A King understands the rules of cosmos.
A King is a person who dwells in many locations.
A King is a person who understands
different dimensions.
A King who is here to help,
who listens for cries for help.

Pleasant manners are his trademark.
He is nonchalant but always caring.
He is ready to help without fearing
any outcome or disability
that may become a liability.

His outlook is of a cheerful manner.
His pleasant manner is ointment
for a hurting Soul.
He is here to stay any evil.
He is a King that is here to help
and listens to every yelp.

A King is equally at home here
and in other dimensions,

at the north pole and on the equator.
Hot and cold is the same. He is a King.

To become a King is a long story
of realizing the potential one has,
realizing the source, the origin,
one's connection to the Higher Self.

Be a King, gentle and understanding.
Rest assured you are a King
if you choose to be.
Rest assured that you are a King
needed by those locked in fear.

MY THEE AND ME

MY THEE AND ME

As a river quivers and flows away
from its source, the source of the river,
we are the river that flows away from its source,
and are becoming the river
that is back on its course.

The river is itself so large
that it will swallow anything on its path
that is in its way. And that day
when the river becomes one with God again
we will be together, together again.

We will be together as one.
We will be together as two that became one.
We will be as those who are the Thee and me.
You and I are the ones who must see
that we become the Thee and me
in one.

In one that is undividable.
In one that is inseparable.
The one who is on her way to freedom
from space and time,
and is flowing into eternity.

Eternity is beckoning to you and me.
Eternity is me who will be joined with my Thee.
Eternity that will become our cradle
that will rock us into the cosmic sleep
of eternal knowledge, and my Thee
and me will not be separated again.

This story is one to be repeated many times.
Many are doing this at these times—
telling the story of awakening humanity
to its eternal freedom,
freedom from time and space.

ILLUSIONS ARE NICE

This illusion is so perfect,
it is a perfect illusion.
It is a perfect, perfect solution
for this world of yours.
For this world of beauty
of rivers, mountains and streams,
for this beauty that you sleep through
in your dreams.

The beauty that is an illusion,
an illusion that can shatter
and will leave you in a state of wonder—
how could I have been so gullible,
so innocent and naïve,
yet so perfect and craving
for my Thee
which is the Thee and me,
in one.
In one entity who we will become,
who we will be once we leave
this spree of illusions.

Illusions are nice. Illusions are pretty.
Illusions are here and sometimes they turn gritty.
Gritty little lives and stories, gritty little tales
that are told over and over again.

Will we ever discover
that these stories are only our perception
of imaginary deception?

Deception of the highest deception possible
as we are not so gullible,
or are we?

Mais oui, mais oui, yes, we are.
We are oh, so gullible.

DISCUSSION WITH MY HIGHER SELF

Eloquently speaking,
I am the one to confide in
as I am you and with élan
many times I helped you
when you were not sure
how to continue on.
Please confide in me.

If you are me, you should know!

Hmm, so you say.
And this is what you believe?

And why not? Why should I not?
If you are me, you know.
I should not need to ask or let you know.

Well, let's explain it better.
I am you, and you are not reporting to me.
You are responsible for yourself
and I am responsible for myself,
but I am also responsible for your wellbeing.
I am your Higher Self. I am your keeper.

Are you aware of me at all times or not?

Hmm, so this is what we will do.
You think of me at all times.
You send me your thoughts and I will reply
whether by an act or directly,
to tell you what it is you need to hear.

Is this clear?

Yes and no.
How is it I am going to hear you, how?
Do I write it down?
Through neglect of writing
I will not have a record.
Through only listening
I may forget some facts.
How do we deal with that?

We will do the following:
listen, and then write a short summary.
Further, it is important to understand
that you need to raise yourself
to another way of communicating.

Yes, I am sending you my thoughts.
Please reply.

I want to spend time writing, being with nature.
I want to be able to help myself and people
through other means
than working for a big corporation.

I want to write, I need to compile what I have.
I don't have that much time
after spending my days at work.
I need to leave my job[3].

---

[3] As much as the author was grateful to her place of employment for her livelihood, she felt it was time to leave. She asked for an early retirement package and was given it, then retired a few months after.

I am financially not able to carry it through
I need your heavenly rapport
in giving visible financial support.

Lord, thank you for getting me out of this rut.
Lord, thank you for helping me to get out.
I am not asking for much.

I need, no, I have,
I have enough finances to carry on.
I am pursuing what I love.
I am on my way to recovery
from constant reincarnations.
I am ready to take off.
I am spreading my wings.

Oh God, thank you for taking care of those things,
my family needs and recreation.
Thank you for giving me enough money
now, in the present, now, now, now.
Thank you God.

THE GATE IS HERE

There was a little girl who did not know
that she was ready to flow,
to flow through the gate of eternity.

The gate is near and is opening
but will be closing again.
This gate is the one that will be closed
after the precession comes to a close,
and then, oops, the moment is gone
and it will take a long time
for it to open again.

This gate is beckoning you and is calling you:
you can, yes, you can.
So do it and charge yourself
to persevere in your meditations,
to persevere in your dedication
to your spiritual Thee.

Your Thee has been waiting quite long.
Your Thee is not impatient as you know,
but your Thee also needs to move on
and without you it cannot execute its plan.

So see how it is connected.
So see how you are affected
by you, your Thee, and others
that are not moving or feeling
that the time is here
that they can glean
other realities.

GET RID OF THE VEIL

A lesson is to believe
that the tree is born with a will to grow leaves.
A lesson is to believe that you are born
to relieve yourself of the responsibility
to be born and born again.

You transgressed against your nature.
You are still a creature
that does not understand reality.
You have not been following your plan
of getting yourself rid of your ignorance of
knowing
that you are a Soul being.

You are one of the Soul beings that
came to Earth to discover the joys of the flesh
and then forgot who you were.
You, as the one who is obedient to your past,
have been trying since then to grasp
all that you could
through the veil of forgetfulness.

Now, now, it is another time.
Now, now, you can do it
if you remember at all times
that you are the one,
that you are a godly being
that lives in eternity.

Please listen very well.
Please work on getting rid of the veil

that is covering us from your view
as we are visible to those
who overcome the ruse
of material reality.

You are a master of the Universe.
You can and ought to be ready
to leave this planet behind,
as this is what you always wanted,
as this is the destiny
for many of you in this century.

YOUR THEE IS WAITING

Your journey is coming to a conclusion.
Emerge from a cocoon,
emerge and fly,
your sojourn is nearing the end.

You are becoming an eternal being
who knows, who realizes,
who is aware
whenever you are on Earth
or other planes.
You are becoming an eternal being
who is aware.

Allow yourself
to touch your everlasting Thee.
You can never leave your Thee—
your Thee is always with you
even if you only knew
that you are an earthly being
and that is all you knew.

Your Thee is waiting to touch your heart.
Your Thee is your everlasting friend.
Your Thee and you, please comprehend,
are one that always was and always will be.
You and your Thee.

Touch your heart and follow your Thee.
Listen to your heart and say:
I am waiting for your cries
to wake me up

and bring me to you in the silence.
You, my Thee, be with me,
be my companion from now on,
on Earth, everywhere,
be my true companion.

Your Thee sits in your heart.
Your Thee is that
which is felt as an enormous heave
when you decide and leave
this Earth.

All seems to come to an end
but it is a beginning of a new stage.

YOU AND I ARE BECOMING ONE

Bliss is coming. Bliss is near.
It is like a breath of air that is clear
of all pollutants and toxins.

We will be one at the Soul level,
you and I, joined together,
you and I, together again.
Oh, do come and ask,
and our God will join us again.

Persevere, please persevere.
Is it becoming clear?
So clear that you are not doubting anymore?
You and I are becoming one.
What could be more fun
than this time that will come
oh, so soon, so soon.

Your cue card is saying,
contemplate, reflect, meditate.
Meditation is what can give you freedom.
Anything that is good,
meditation makes even better.

Your house will be our house.
Your house will be God's house.
Your house will be clean and ready
to welcome me.
Me, who is your Thee, a Thee who is me.
Me, who is so happy to be joined with Thee.

We will become an entity
that is ready to create a new life,
a new life that will again reincarnate
and will one day become its own entity.

So, that is a cycle of eternity—
an entity that gives life,
life that becomes an entity and so on.
Rejoice, that time will be here soon,
your Thee is waiting
for this eternal moment of joy and bloom.

SO THIS IS HOW YOU WONDER

The Universe will not paint a rosy picture
as you are the one who is painting
and then may be panting
as the picture is slanting
toward a scenario
that is not to your liking.

You are a King.
Do you know what it means?
It means you can fly.
You can traverse local and foreign spaces.
You can traverse throughout the Universes
at your will.

Locally speaking,
all is visible and green.
Mountains are beautiful,
so is the evergreen.
Elephants are grazing in Africa,
mammoths are in ice caves waiting,
mammals are evolving
to experience humanity.

All is the way it should be,
but there is this little, little Thee
that is you that is wondering:
Where do I fit? Where do I go?
Where do I change to have what I want?
Where do I cross to eternity and back?
Where do I see my enchanted guides
and hear their whispers?

Where do I enthral myself with their wisdom?
Where, when, when, where?
Please let me know.

So this is how you wonder,
this is how you wonder.
All is the way it should be.
All is well as it can be.
Otherwise, you would not be.
You would not be
and your Thee would not be.

But as you are, there is a calling
that needs to be fulfilled—
your calling to live fully
as a Soul being.

As a Soul being that is fully aware,
that it is not afraid
to triumphantly proclaim
I am a Thee, yes I am.

ONENESS

YOU ARE A ONENESS BEING

Apropos, who are you?
Are you of the Earth or are you of Heaven?
Are you a poet or are you a heathen?
Are you a girl or are you a boy?
Are you someone who does not know?

You are all, a boy and a girl.
One who cares and does not care.
As all is encompassed in one,
as all is not what you know
here on this Earth.

Your state of mind is liable
for the outcome of the reality
that envelopes you to the point
that you are no longer a hybrid,
that you are not anymore
an animal and a Soul
but you are a oneness being
who can operate on all levels,
who can push and pull,
be glad and happy
and be aware of her powers,
who is a master and a slave
at the same, the very same time.

What is it we are talking about?
It is duality congealed in oneness.
It is a feeling of unity with God.
It is a feeling overpowering you
when your guide is actually you.

You are your guide.
You are your teacher.
You can outline your lessons
and you can teach them, as well.
All is one.

Understand that all is one,
one is all.
What does it mean? What is all?
All is big and small.
It is beautiful and not so beautiful.
It is. It is what it is and that is all.

We all are not only here.
We are everywhere.
We are flowers. We are birds.
We are talkers. We are hawkers.
We are all, small, large, beautiful.
We are all.

We are one.
We respect each other,
we are one.

WAKE UP FROM YOUR DREAM

Wake up from your dream.
Your dream is coming to an end.
Your dream is coming to a close.
You will wake and will dance with us,
sing our universal song,
the song of love and understanding.

Please come home, come home.
We are ready to see you to your glory.
We are ready to pick you up
when you feel sorry,
sorry for yourself and others
that are so near and yet far
from becoming a star
that is shining ever so bright.

You will be our last charge,
as we are getting ready at large
to become bound for another reality.
Our reality, as we speak,
is getting built by our ancestors
who can do what we cannot.

So, you see, you and your Thee,
all is relative.
As you are always thinking and weighing
what we are sending you,
we are thinking and weighing
what they are sending us.
They are our brothers and sisters.
They are our ancestors.

Persevere, persevere.
Perseverance is the blessing.
Perseverance is the dressing
on the salad of life.
The salad of agony, of happiness,
of trials and triumphs,
of medleys unknown to us.

You are eager to listen
as you are sitting in your prison
of your earthly body.
That body that is magnificent
as it is a high achievement
of a power that comes from God.

Our God is your God.
Our Universe is your Universe.
Our mind is your mind.
Our happiness is your happiness.
We are one. We will stay one
and we plead to be always one.

Your bliss is our bliss.
Your happiness is our happiness.
Your world is our world.
Your thought is our thought
as we are one.
We are one.

THAT BIG SEA

Mais oui, mais oui, all is gone.
All that needs to change is done.
All that is perplexed and not moving,
all that is sliding and folding,
all that is not in flex
and is in the vex,
all that is going to go.

All that is going to go,
to remove the stagnation,
to elevate humanity,
to bring excitement,
to bring clarity,
to bring a natural Light
into your being soon.

During your sojourn
many other people
will live and die.
Many other people
will encounter each other.
During your sojourn
you will be in the center of it all.

As soon as you can see
and identify yourself
as a part of that big, big "sea"
then you can see
that you all are one.

As soon as that happens
you will bring yourself
from forgetfulness.

You are coming out
from the loneliness and the separation
and you will be with others
to experience your renewed oneness—
your becoming one.

DISCOURSE ON CAMARADERIE

Alas, this discourse is on camaraderie.
This discourse is on becoming one.
This discourse is of importance to you and all,
as you and others
need to leave their aloneness atoll.

Aloneness is a way
of identifying yourself with yourself.
Aloneness is a sign of who you are
without relating to others.

This stage is about becoming large.
At this point, it does not matter who you are
or what age you are.

At this point your being wakes up
from the loneliness stupor
and looks above to find another Soul
that is like you, that is an extension.

This extension is then connected to you
and the process becomes that you
will be one with the extended Soul.
Your extended self is in a state of flux
and is dealing on its level with the rest.

Therefore, you all are then a part of each other.
Therefore, you all can be a mass
where each is individual.

You all can be a mass
that breathes as one,
that lives and pushes on
as one large entity.

This discourse is not finished yet.
However, we feel
this beginning is all you need
to comprehend how it is
that you become one.

WE ARE ONE BIG SOUL

You are ready to move to another plane.
You are ready to enjoy and to migrate
to other dimensions
by expanding your consciousness.
You are ready to let go
of your earthly ties.

You are ready to say:

Here I come.
I am multidimensional.
I am ready to soar.
I am ready to uphold all—
all I need to do and know,
all that is dear to my heart,
that is close to me,
that is available,
that is of me and of others,
that is our Soul imprint from Heaven,
from God, from our maker.

You are ready.
You need to move on
and you are also perplexed
as to what it may mean,
as you are steeped in your understanding
of the third dimension but not of the others.

You and your loved ones are here on Earth
to find out how we can all co-operate
on all existing planes.

If you cannot reach beyond your plane
then you will not be able to help and to claim
that you understand what it means
that we all are multidimensional,
that you live where you are
and you also travel
whenever you are drawn to
by your Soul design,
as you know when and how
this needs to be done.

You are able to soar.
You are able to let go.
You are able to visit places.
You are able to qualify for "flying classes".
And yes, you earned your stripes.
The time is coming and you will understand.
You will be able to travel over the Earth
and come back whenever you desire.

You will come
and you will not need to take a tram,
as you will be able to propel yourself
effortlessly and eloquently,
ultimately always with yourself,
for yourself and then for others.

As what is it we are?
We are one big Soul.
We are one Soul that breathes and lives.
We are God that came alive on all planes
created by him.

Those planes are full of joy and of beauty
and you can have them all—
your world and others.
That is exactly what ascended masters
mastered millennia ago.

DUALITY IS ON THE WAY OUT

You will recover from your unanimity
with all that is not totally godly.
You will break away
from pettiness, jealousy,
from mundane thoughts,
from needless fights.

All is in your hands,
God just observes.
You are the maker of your Universe.

Rest assured all is well.
All is the way it is expected to be—
dreary and beautiful, nasty and nice,
naughty and right, righteous and wrong,
bright and dark, day and night.
Duality. Mais oui, mais oui,
all duality is on the way out!

Duality is of a rendered past.
As you are casting the net
and raising the mast
and are skimming across
the ocean of eternity,
you are grateful to leave and find
that duality no longer applies.

Duality is mass consciousness
gelled into matter.
Duality is mass consciousness
that stopped believing

that by leaving duality behind
the world of Spirits is open to us.
The world of starry beings is a possibility,
and so is reclamation of the right to live
and believe that one might
be what one is—a Soul.

Abracadabra it is not—
duality is on the way out.

THIS RUSE CALLED DUALITY

Without low, you cannot be high.
Without hate, you cannot see love.
Without dark, you won't understand light.

Duality is real,
unless you will believe
that duality is not.

Duality is only for the folks
who cannot get away from a notion
that they always will be drinking from the potion
of hate and love, of day and night,
of all negative and positive sides
that are called duality.

See through this ruse called duality.
Become one
who is spiritually advanced enough
to cross the barrier that is invisible,
the barrier between us and you,
the barrier that can be flipped away
with a flick of a small finger.

Please do have that wisdom
to see through duality.
Please be wise, please be nimble.
Get rid of your thimble
that keeps you imprisoned,
that is so heavy that you cannot levy
your thoughts as you should.

Duality is not real.
It is just your fear
that keeps you here.
It is, any way you look,
your choice of doing things by the book
or being yourself!

A pleading end to this story—
ask yourself, who am I?
And you will get an answer,
you will be rewarded by losing your burden,
you will fly as a bird
to celebrate your rebirth.
You will, you will.

Please wake up and become one.
One, who is in tune with your omnipotent Soul,
one, who is worshipping your own goal
which is to become one.

One, as in one singularity.
One, as in one, no plurality.
One, as in one, no duality.
As in one who is omnipotent
and puts his burden down
on a vehicle that starts on its way
and comes home without a burden.

Oh, please wake up!

YOUR SOJOURN

YOUR SOJOURN IS PLANNED BY YOU

If you are a little girl,
don't you wish for a blue sky?
Don't you wish to know who you are?
And if you are a grown up woman,
don't you ask yourself
who you are again?

These thoughts are a perpetual wish,
and then answers come in a swoosh and swish
to enlighten you with your truth.
But those truths can be somewhat different,
as the truths are based on what you are at the time.

Your sojourn is nearing the end.
Please comprehend
that the sojourn is planned
and executed by you,
therefore the plan is known to you.

The plan is as follows:
Forget who you are
as you see yourself today.
You are not an earthling forever,
and moreover, you all were,
and always will be, a Spirit.

Your earthly clothes are of flesh and diseases,
of troubles and questions, of joys and pleasures,
of good food and wine, of robberies and wars,
of all that which you attract
to yourself.

Humanity is in the depths of calamity,
as humanity is not listening to God.
Humanity is going down the wrong street,
the world should be round but it is oblique.
The world should be round
and should stay that way,
as the circle becomes a spiral going upward,
and the oblique is not, it is not that way.

Your sojourn is nearing the end.
Please comprehend
that the sojourn is planned
and executed by you.

YOUR JOURNEY

The stars are bright and the flight
of earthly reincarnations is nearing the end.
You are a child of the Universe.
You, as a child, were born and raised,
and then you struck out on your own.

You traveled through time.
You traveled through space.
You traveled in time,
and in time you came back
to be born again and again.

You then understood less and less,
as you started forgetting
and got yourself in a mess,
in multiple reincarnations,
adorning yourself with jewels,
also believing in scarcity and strange rituals.

The more cycles you did,
the less you knew about where you came from.
You did not remember who you were
and you did not follow the goal to where
you wanted to end up traveling.

You did all. You educated yourself
and now you are ready to wean yourself
from the earthly influences,
from the third dimension,
from all that is not spiritually based.

And you can. You can at last
invite yourself and pass
through the gate of reckoning
that is beckoning from afar,
that is beckoning and is open to all
who are striving to search out the Light
that is a Source and has all the might
of God ingrained in itself.

Your journey is getting to the point
where you can join the angelic realm,
your guides, your ministers
who have been ministering to you
throughout millennia.

Your journey on Earth is coming to an end.

WHAT COLOURS ARE YOURS?

Life is not a mystery, it is not.
Life is a song that you sing
and only you can make your life appear
to be white or black,
or all colours.

What colours are yours, which are yours?
Is it white or black? Which is it?
It is not very easy to distinguish, you say?
Oh, well, did not we say
that you are your destiny maker?

The destiny maker needs to recognize the colours.
The destiny maker is the one who paints them.
The destiny maker knows how to apply them.
The destiny maker is a decisive factor
and also is a benefactor
of all good and not so good he created.

Make your song a story where you benefit,
where you will be outfitted
with a new dress and clothes,
with a new thought,
and then, well then,
you will be ready
to continue your journey again.

RECEIVE LIGHT

Light is the name of God's presence.
Light is a Saint's glory.
It is a satisfied appetite
filled with dew and honey.
It is when you breathe the air
filled with love and compassion.

Your air is filling with Light.
The day is near when all will become bright.
Dark one day and then
it will continue to grow in the Light intensity,
and all will be shiny and full of Light.

The day of reckoning is near.
All will see the Light on the horizon
but not all will continue to receive it,
as not all are able to hold it.

The ones who receive Light will not fight,
will not strive any more to live in this world
but will continue their journey
elsewhere.

BELIEVE IT AND YOU WILL SEE IT

It was as it was.
It will be as it will be...
Not so, it was as you wanted
and it will be as you make it.

During your sojourn things will happen,
roses and thorns, dual roles.
Best of all is what you believe.
If you cannot believe, it will not be,
it will not be for you, even if it exists.

So, the lesson is about you believing—
your seeing depends on you.
It is not that it does not exist,
it is not that it is non-existent,
it is your rendering,
it is your perceiving,
it is you.

If you cannot believe, it is not.
If you can, then it is.
Alas, believe it then you will see it.
See, open your eyes—
being open to believing is a virtue
and not being open is not.

Sometimes, if you don't believe,
it is a way of saying, I cannot learn.
Sometimes, it is a way of saying, I don't care.
Sometimes, it is a way of saying, I learned
and my journey changed.

ALL IS TAKEN TO A NEW STATE

During your sojourn,
you meet like-minded people
and you befriend them,
and they befriend you.

During your sojourn,
all will happen as planned.
During your sojourn,
all will be explained.
During your sojourn,
all is taken to a new state.

All that is on your mind will be discussed.
All that is examined will be learned.
All that is not wanted will be brushed away.
All that is, will be known.
All that is not, will be known, as well.

All will become one.
All will unravel itself
into a bigger entity of Thy Thee.

During your sojourn, all will be explained,
all will be experienced, all will be accosted,
all will be surrendered,
all will be.

SOJOURNS ARE NEARING THE END

Your sojourn is nearing the end.
Eternal life is becoming the norm
on the level of the being who is aware,
who is aware of herself
on all levels.

Awareness is a state
when you are aware of before, after and now.
When you become one who K N O W S,
who knows, who knows.

Sullen looks out, gleaming faces in.
Desperation out, happiness in.
Ignorance superseded by caring.
Banality superseded by being thoughtful.
Inaccuracy superseded by being accurate.

No more doubts, fears, predicaments.
Changes are coming. You will be heading
toward an extinction of the way
you are today.

No more predicaments about your sexuality.
No more predicaments about your individuality.
Doubts, fears will disappear.

God is speaking.
Soul design is unravelling to its potential.
It is opening as a lotus, as a lotus flower
that is white, strong, and belongs to all.

All feel the petals opening.
All feel the meadow growing,
the scent of a flower becoming the smell
that is eternally embedded in all.

The scent of nature, the scent of being...
Sojourning, living, loving.

COMING HOME

THOSE WHO KNOW

"Derelicts" are coming home.
Derelicts may sound too intimidating.
Let's change the name and let's be daring.
Let's say those who know are coming home.

Those who know are returning home.
They left their nest to experience matter,
and came to a halt wondering, who are we?
Who is it under this skin and flesh,
who is it, who?

Those who know are returning home,
those who know that their skin and bone
are not all, that there is a Spirit,
and the Spirit is calling them home.

Spirit is calling:
I am yours to have, I am yours.
You are me, and I am you.

Those who woke up and remembered
are coming home,
as they recognized their yearning for more.
Yearning for more of their real self,
more of their spiritual wealth,
more of their exuberant Self.

More of their analogical fight for their freedom.
Freedom from oppression of themselves,
freedom from dilly-dallying,
freedom, freedom.

Best of all is to come, best of all is here.
Best of all, do not forget
you are a spiritual being.
You are a spiritual being first,
then you are the rest.

Your ability to comprehend
who you are is not that far.
Do as we say, contemplate, meditate,
and you will lift that veil,
veil of forgetfulness.

Those who know are returning home.

PRAYER OF THE PRODIGAL DAUGHTER

Please clear me of all encumbrances.
Please clear me, give me a chance
to be briefed. Be kind
and send me your blessing all the time.

I need your support as never before,
as I am in a stupor of disbelief.
I want to turn another leaf,
the leaf that can help me to find myself.

Help me to find myself
and be one with myself.
Do explain what to do,
help me find my new you.

Do help and clear me
from this suffering
of not knowing who I am.
Help me to get to the end of my search
where all comes together,
where you and I can talk again
about our previous times
when we felt like one.

Like a bird that can fly,
like a bird who can cry,
cry a victorious cry of knowing
that soaring is all they need to do.

Soaring below and above the clouds,
clouds that are heavy,

but they don't matter.
They are just dewy,
very dewy physical matter.

Help me to climb up from my abyss,
from my forgetfulness.
Please do it gently,
so as not to scare me.
Please do it skilfully,
so as not to frighten me.

I can be frightened and I can be bad.
I can be lovely and I can be sad.
I am looking for companionship,
I am looking for camaraderie
that can blossom into a sistership,
that can blossom into a relationship.

I hope that you care.
I hope that you can be so kind to me
that we will understand each other really well
to the point of such closeness
that we will be inseparable.

Inseparable in our views.
Inseparable in our news
that we will be sharing with each other,
that we will be treasuring forever.

Oh, my God within, will you help me?
Help me to realize
that God's glory is ours to share
with all other creatures on this Earth.

DO COME HOME

To be or not to be,
that is the question.
To be or not to be.
What is it going to be?
You will be what you will be,
no doubt about that.

We are here to call on you,
as we want to be with you.
We are your brothers and sisters,
we are your ancestors.
We are your guides and angels.
We are simply yours.
We are forever together.

Please come home.
We are missing you,
we, your brothers and sisters,
yours near and dear
who are here
waiting for you,
you who are lost
and looking for the past
that will connect to the future.

Home is where you feel at home.
Home is your sweet, beautiful gown,
gown of planets and stars.
Those stars that are glitters in your eyes,
those stars that are so high and shiny,
yes, they are.

Please do come home.
We will speak to you
and sing your favourite songs.
We will nourish you and present you
with Universe bonbons
of love and light and understanding.

CLOSE IS YOUR BEING FREED

Visible is easy to comprehend.
Invisible is of a secretive nature.
Invisible is of a godly stature
as it is of gods and goddesses,
of universal love,
of stars and galaxies,
of all that is afar,
that is afar and yet so close.

Close is your everlasting peace.
Close is your being freed
from your earthly ties.
Close is your mesmerised look into the future.
Close is your angelic growth.
Close is your evangelic searching
for truth and freedom.

It is about the consciousness expansion.
It is about the realization
that you are omnipotent,
that you are one,
that you are God.

You are not of earthly matter,
that is only your today's garb
that is only temporary,
but you and others
are gods that live on Earth now.

THESE ARE EXCITING TIMES

These are exciting times,
as you will en masse
reach the universal consciousness.
The best times are still to come
and it all will be so effortless
that you will be surprised
to find out that yes,
to do it en masse
is not a difficult task.

It is a fellowship that will lift you up.
It will be a glorious event.
It will be a consciousness shift
that will lift many, many,
into other realms.

You will be able to listen to our voices.
You will be able to walk with us in our gardens.
You will be able to sing in our chorus.
You will be with us, your true family.

We have been where you are today.
Some of us, though, have chosen another way.
And some of us are of a different structure
altogether.

However, these are just the outer signs.
We all are one big mass
of Souls that are not divided
the way you feel divided on Earth.

These times are coming and are exciting
as mass consciousness is lifting
and the new vibrations are coming
that will transform the whole Earth.

Without a vibrational change
no new things can come to life.
No new worlds can open.
No evolution will take place.
No new gardens will be created.
These are exciting times.

Project the image of love at all times
as this is needed for human beings
to evolve to another reality,
where the vibrations are higher,
where the vibrations are acquired
through loving all your kind.

THAT IS GOD OF THE PAST

Those who know are coming home.
You are reluctantly, and some of you joyfully,
discovering your origin.
You are not without doubts,
you are not without turmoil.

Derelicts are those who forgot.
You forgot where you came from.
Every reincarnation is new to you.
You forgot who you were before the lifetime
you are living on the Earth today.

You don't remember your origins.
You have forgotten who you are
through many, many reincarnations
that have continuously wiped your mind.

Today, you are not looking for a harness anymore.
You are not seeking disturbances.
You are prepared to accept God,
God within yourself.

A fable says:
I am God and you will have no other gods to serve.
I am God and you are not to have the nerve
to question me.

Well, that is a God of the past,
that is a God that you must, must leave behind.
That God of yours that you had for centuries
is a figure of your fears. Leave that God behind.

WE ALL ARE CONNECTED

We all are strongly connected.
We are one big, boiling, appreciating mass
that is developing its consciousness
to the point of understanding
who we are.

And then, once we understand,
some of us will come home,
and some of us will be given
a slightly different role.
We will lift ourselves and go
to another level of existence.

Know that if one grows and learns,
all grow and learn,
as we all are one, one glorious one,
who is an expression of God.

You may ask, and who is that God,
who is that omnipotent being?
He is an intelligent primordial energy
that flows and bubbles and turns
and twists and feels.
God is, was and will be.

YOU ARE
FROM THE STARS

AN ANGEL FALLEN FROM THE SKY

Understand who you are.
You are an angel fallen from the sky.
You are living proof of accepting
earthly life to the point of forgetting
that you are, and always will be,
a creator with God of your life.

Be yourself, and bring yourself
to the point of acceptance and say:

Yes, I know who I am.
Yes, I know who they are.
I am my own chief and guide
and I created what I live.
I am my very own chief,
no one else has the power over me
to decide what will happen to me,
just myself.

Then do what needs to be done.
Begin. Begin to be your own boss
by creating your own life story,
instead of waiting for someone to say,
oh, yes, do it this way.

Entirely different scenarios
will weave their ways throughout your life
when you decide your fate.
You are the decider, you are the maker,
you are the author of your own life story.

You are the best judge
of what you need and where you need to be,
and that should always be,
that should always be the scenario.

The scenario is simple.
Laugh, and you will see a dimple.
Smile, and smiles will be given to you.
Cry, and you will see the tears.
Ask, and you will receive.
Appreciate, and you will be appreciated.
Lose control, and you will not be at the helm.
Applaud, and you will be applauded.

YOUR CORE IS LIGHT

A starry being is star matter
that shines to live,
that shines to breathe,
that is Light itself
that is shining throughout eternity.

Star matter that is not blocked in knowing
that life is a blessed event,
that life is a continuous stream
of starry eyed, everlasting
starry beings.

You are asking, and what is it they do?
They don't do, they are.
They are beacons of Light
that is shimmering and is bright,
that is shining throughout millennia
sending messages of peace and love.
They are Light Beings
whose life consists of being Light.

Starry beings.
They are peacekeepers on the Earth.
They are peacekeepers of the Universe.
They are messengers of love.
Their core being is Light.

This Light travels to all and nowhere.
This Light is and casts no shadow.
This Light acts as a catalyst
to bring more life forward.

This Light is an enabler of God.
This Light is a protector of those
who call, who need it the most.
This Light embalms you in a protective shield.
This Light is a life-giving substance.

This Light permeates the universal eternity.
This Light brings life and opens doors
to those who seek Light, not dark.
Who seek enlightenment
and are seeking an explanation
of their evolution,
as they sometimes forget who they are.

This Light is a warm feeling in your chest
when you are happy.
This Light is a knowing that you belong,
that you are a creator with God,
that you can transmit yourself in a blink
from here to there and back
to experience all that which is a quark[4].

---

[4] A quark is a very small particle that makes up protons and
neutrons in the atomic nucleus.

LIGHT IS KNOWLEDGE

Send yourself the Light,
the Light is what you need.
Be aware of the Light close to you,
be aware of the Light shining on you.

Send yourself the Light
to give you an understanding
of the Light being around you
and understanding
that you are responsible
for keeping the Light glowing,
ever so brightly glowing.

The Light is knowledge.
The Light is warmth.
The Light is necessary for the growth
of humans and plants,
and all living things.
This is a law
that cannot be broken and ignored.

This Light we are talking about
is the Light that is of a different sight.
It is not a Light to be seen with the naked eye.
It is a Light that is to be understood
with your inner perception,
with your inner vision.

The Light, that life-giving property
is of a nourishing quality,
is a nurturing and beholding Light

123

that is bright and warm,
that is knowing you and all,
that can speak within as an intelligence,
that is the base of your Universe
and other worlds and Universes.

WE ARE CONNECTED BY LIGHT

The Light was born from a word.
There was a sound, Aum.
The sound grew and needed a partner,
therefore it developed into
an entity of Light proportions.[5]
This entity needed further company,
this entity was not ready
to continue living with sound only.

This entity persuaded the sound
to mate further and then they created
an offspring called human.
This human was an evolutionary product
of all that happened before and after.
The evolution was of a lengthy matter.

The evolution is not finished,
as nothing ever will be complete.
All will be in a way of flexing and changing.
All will be in a way of productive researching.
Asking, hmm, what is it we need to do
to come to point B
from where we are today,
and where we will be
when we reach that new point
in our lives the next day.

---

[5] There is a direct relationship between sound and light. If you speed up sound's frequency, you come up with a frequency of light; light is speeded up sound, and sound is slowed down light.

We are all connected by the Light.
The Light is threading throughout.
Throughout our bodies,
throughout our offspring, our grass,
our Earth, our rivers, and so on.

The thread of Light is a link
that is important,
as genetic material is travelling
through this link
on and on.

It is important to experience the Light
in its fullness and delight,
as it should be a delight
and should always feel right.
The Light.

UNEARTH YOUR STARRY ORIGINS

Once upon a time, there was a girl.
This girl was not of matter.
This girl was not of this world.
This girl was a curious being
and she decided to come out
and start trying
other coats of realities.

She, as a starry being,
did not possess a sense
of liking and disliking,
sense of good and bad,
sense of feeling warmth and cold.
She was a starry being
who was just that, a star.

A star that shone throughout millennia,
a star who was to give Light.
As a starry being, she was obliged
to take precautions
and avoid a collision
with dense matter.

But she, as a curious being
decided to jump
and start observing
other realities and their natures.

She, as a starry being, primordial mass,
delinquent, as she was,
she left her brood of starry beings,

trying hard to decipher other types of being
and became involved with earthly matter.

Earthly matter has its own charms,
its own trials, and this starry girl
decided to stay there,
and the Earth became her station.

It is you, isn't it?
You had enough grit
to discover your real origins
that are coming, coming
to the surface of your memories,
memories of your past.

You, as a starry being
are drawn to other starry beings.
You, as a starry being
are drawn to those
who like you are on a quest
to discover, to unearth
their past, their present
and future, as starry beings.

THE BEAST IS SUBSIDING

The nature of things is given at birth,
being of a starry origin or an earthly origin.

Your make-up is matter
that congealed and became heavy.
Your origin was more dewy,
more liquidy, more spiritual,
more contrasting
to what you are today.

What you are today
is recognized as a chameleon.
It is you changing from starry to earthly,
from earthly to starry again.

This can be a game.
This can be a serious undertaking.
This is your choice. This is your making.
You can and you are getting back
to your starry origins.

Starry being within you
is waiting to be brought out,
is waiting for an occasion to pop
to the surface and be on top,
on top of all that happens,
of all that transpires,
of all.

Starry being within you is your nature.
The beast is subsiding

and is getting smaller.
Your starry eyes can see far.
Your starry ears can hear a lot.
Your starry mouth pronounces syllables
that have been uttered way, way back
when you were together
and were talking to each other
in starry languages.

THE EXPERIMENT GOES ON

Mesmerizing is the thought
that you are not aware of your origins.
Origins that stem from far, far back,
origins that are so "enchanting".

You are a starry being.
You are of stardust.
You are of a starry consciousness
that is not a thing of the past.
You are a starry, starry being.

Prodigal daughters and sons
are coming home.
But are all of starry origins?

Well, here it is. It goes like this:
Before Adam and Eve,
before any human origins,
the starry beings inhabited this planet
to create and cohabit the Earth.

And the venture started to solidify.
And the venture became the norm.
Starry beings, not creation,
became earthlings.

They became a brood of their own,
with their own history, their own laws.
They kept on forgetting who they were.
Then one day a new starry being came
and all started coming back.

Was it Christ?
There were other starry beings before.
Christ was the one
who brought all together
by his insistent proclamation
that he was a son of God, and so on.
You know the story, or at least you should.

Starry beings that inhabited this planet
and then turned earthlings
were not the original occupants.
Original occupants were microscopic.
Later came dinosaurs, apes and such.
Those were beings that lived on this planet.

Starry beings became involved
in a cross breeding
and became involved in experimenting.
They made the starry being into a human being.

By experimenting,
they lost their own consciousness.
By experimenting, they became the experiment.
They lost their vision. They lost their own Soul
to the experiment that goes on and on.

Throughout the millennia the starry beings
have been mixing the genes,
mixing the consciousness,
preparing a new breed of people
who will experiment on themselves,
to become the starry beings again.

The cycle goes on and on.
They are sort of a clan
that experiments, and then learns
through living as an experiment as well.

You are a starry being.
You came here a long time ago.
Your name is of old origins.
Your name signifies progress and beauty.
Your name is an old, old name.

You can reach out and touch
other starry beings by saying:
I am a starry being.
I have forgotten how to reach out to you
and communicate.
I am here and waiting for you
to help me open the gate.

The gate that will be the squeezing point
for those who squeeze through it
and literally open their eyes
to see the other side.

You are a starry being.

YOU ARE VERY SPECIAL

Listen to the wind as it whistles through the trees.
Listen to your voice as it quivers in your bliss.
Bliss of knowing that it is here,
that your freedom is near,
your freedom that is coming soon.

You will be able to fly to the moon
and you will not be an astronaut,
and this flying is what you want.

A flight that is effortless
as you are hurtling through space,
through the space of your freedom
that is beckoning to you from within.

From within you, as you are vast
as the vastest Universe,
as you are its exact inner image,
so explore it.

Lose your three dimensional feeling
of heavy gravity and leaden boots
that keep you grounded to your roots
on this Earth.

On this Earth that is only your temporary station,
as you all are here on probation
that will last until you understand
that you are not creatures of this Earth.

You are special, very special.
You are of us who are your vessel.
You are of us, your star companions.

As you hurtle through space to meet us,
we will await you until you greet us
with the understanding shown on your faces
that your deliverance is here
and that you are all to us very dear.

So dear that we quiver with excitement
and we are waiting patiently for the moment
when all sisters and brothers
will be with us again.

THE GUIDES ARE AT YOUR SIDE

Mais oui, mais oui, we are here again.
Mais oui, mais oui, here is what we came to say:

You are the one who became an earthling
a long time ago.
We see your toiling. We see your rejoicing.
We see you committing yourself to the plane
that is not your home.

Come to us again.
Come to us to live with us,
with us who are born in the stars,
with us who are born without pain and cries.

We are the ones who are unlimited.
We are the ones, who like you,
have always existed.
The time is ripe
for you to attempt to rejoin us.
If that is what you want, we are here to help.

Your life will be long and healthy,
and you will have time aplenty
to work with us and decide
that we are the ones who will be,
as you call us, your guides.

The guides, who are always at your side
as you are always at the side
of your own children,
as we all are children of the Universe.

We beckon to you as one of us
to come and join us
on your way to the unspeakable heights
of unbelievable beauty and bliss.

So, what is it you are going to do?
Is it the earthly life over and over again?
If not, what are your choices?
It is your move and for us to see
what your next move is.

And that is why we are here
to lift you up here, up here,
where angels play and cavort,
where grass is blue and red,
where songs are written and read,
where all is as it is and is created as new,
as the morning dew and the evening scent
of a new beginning of the next day.

READY TO JUMP THE BERTH

Elaborate lies do not pay,
dishonesty does not bring fruits,
lethargy can kill—
during your sojourn,
you will experience all.
During your sojourn,
you will encounter all life situations.

During your sojourn,
lessons are experienced,
elementary and special truths are reviewed.
During your journey, all happens to you
until you come back and return.

This is not about sainthood.
This is not about rapture.
This is about a meaningful evolution
that will take you to a new resolution,
when you decide to forgo what you have
and follow that what you are looking for.

One day you will discover your true self.
One day you will realize who you are.
You will sprout a new hope
that will grow and grow
and will diligently pursue the real you.

Acclaim your past.
Acclaim your present.
Your future is already done.
Your future is already here.

Your future is happening as we speak.
Your future is all that is yours.
Your future is yours to have.

During your sojourn
all will be clarified.
All boundaries will be delimited.
All will be ready to fall into a pattern,
a pattern of mundane
but also exciting
when you recognize
that you are a star being.

A star being that is from the stars
living on Earth,
that is ready to jump the berth,
that is ready to look up and say
here I come my brothers and sisters,
my brethren.
Here I am, here I am.

THE BIVOUAC

The bivouac is not the place to live in.
The bivouac is a constricting place
that can be warm for a stage
when you require that sense of security.

Then there is the next step when you realize
that your cozy bivouac is a constriction.
You break the walls to feel free,
then you live and expand to the degree
that the process starts again.

Your new bivouac becomes small
and you see that it is an atoll
of loneliness and forgetfulness,
so you break down the walls again.

Through this process you eliminate
the hardship, the hatred and so on,
until you reach the cocoon for the last time
and you fly out to live as a Light Being
who has no limits, no bivouacs.

You are a star, starry, starry being.
Your curious nature is a thing of the past,
as you raised the mast and you are traveling
the oceans you traveled before.
You became a creature that knows
and therefore what was curious
was interchanged with knowing.

Knowing does not mean you are not seeking.
Knowing is the stage where curiosity
is not needed any more,
and seeking is what propels you further,
further, on and on.

PRENATAL MEMORIES ARE RESURFACING

During your sojourn, you are blessed.
You are blessed by a Saint
that is within you. You are blessed
because of the nature of your being,
because of the creature that is living
in you.

That creature
is of an earthly and also spiritual nature.
The creature, you,
is awakening to the true blue sky,
the true spiritual being, you.

All is well.
Beast within you is not that swell.
It is roaring, it is standing up,
it is belligerently doing so,
as it is not ready to give up,
as it is not ready to serve,
it is not ready to be.

To be as a starry being
is to be aware of all goings on
within and without.
Starry being is of matter and of thought.
Starry being is of one Soul
with other starry beings who are.

Who are beings who are.
Who are beings who were.
Who are beings who clue others.

Who are beings who press others.
Who are beings who help others.

Abracadabra it ain't,
sojourn of the flightless bird is at the end.
Prenatal memories are resurfacing.
They are dwelling on the starry origin
of you, of all that are here on the Earth
that are awakening to the past
of being starry beings.

Long sojourn is coming to an end.
It has achieved what was needed,
it has achieved what was wanted.
It learned, it figured out,
it pushed and pulled.

It obliterated mundane thought.
It brought liberating feeling
to all that could not believe,
to those still reeling from discovering
that their starry origin
is a fact of their lives.

YOU ARE FOREIGN TO THE EARTH

Pleasant is your life this lifetime.
You say, how about the others?
What transpired?
Was I happy? Was I sad?

You were happy and unhappy.
You were unpleasant and pleasant.
You were not too rich and you were very rich.
You were of all different upbringings.

Your home is at the stars.
You are that primordial mass
that evolved and started looking
for other places to help honing,
to help honing your skills.
You are the stars, not the flesh bodies.
You are welcome to return any time.

Stars were your breeding ground
where you learned that the way of life
is the spiritual way, that the Earth is matter
that is experienced but then is left behind.
All experiences are then recounted:
what was, what you learned and remembered,
what will become.

This does not suggest time.
This does not suggest that experience is linear.
This suggests that you are ready
to find your way back
to where you originated eons ago.

Bliss is when you realize
that you are foreign to the Earth,
that you lived there many times,
that your origins are the stars,
that you do not become whole
until you know
who you are.

In knowing, there is might.
In knowing, there is power.

ABOUT THE AUTHOR

Helena Kalivoda is devoted to sharing "heavenly" messages that support readers in transforming their lives. Lives of peace and happiness are available to those who learn the power of creation through an open heart as encouraged by Helena's books.

AWAKEN! Spirit Is Calling, Helena's first book, contains powerful truths for each person's journey. These poignant teachings were downloaded from Helena's guides and angels. Be prepared for your "aha" moments when reading the book.

Her second book, *WAKE UP! Your Heart Is Calling*, leads readers to realize that all aspects of humanity, when denied pure love, are bound to eventually fail and cannot be healthy. This book connects to an online environment where you can access extended resources to help you apply the learned principles.

WAKE UP! Prosperity Is Calling, Helena's third book, outlines The Seven Principles to Living a Life of Prosperity. These principles will become your truth and experience once you use them and live them consistently.

Currently, Helena is working on a new series of *Purposeful Mind* books of poetry. This book, *Illumination,* is the second book of this series.

Helena holds a BA in Economics and B.Sc. in Computer Science. She is a mother of three, living in Canada. In 1997, she left the corporate world to continue the writing she started in the early nineties.

Visit www.awakenbyhelena.ca for more information about Helena Kalivoda's books.